Tom Brady

A Football Star
Who Cares

Barry Wilner

Enslow Elementary
an imprint of

E | **Enslow Publishers, Inc.**
40 Industrial Road
Box 398
Berkeley Heights, NJ 07922
USA

http://www.enslow.com

Enslow Elementary, an imprint of Enslow Publishers, Inc.

Enslow Elementary® is a registered trademark of Enslow Publishers, Inc.

Library of Congress Cataloging-in-Publication Data

Wilner, Barry.
  Tom Brady : a football star who cares / Barry Wilner.
     p. cm. — (Sports stars who care)
  Includes bibliographical references and index.
  Summary: "A biography of football player Tom Brady,
highlighting his charitable work"—Provided by publisher.
  ISBN 978-0-7660-3773-1
  1. Brady, Tom, 1977—Juvenile literature. 2. Football players—United States—Biography—
Juvenile literature. 3. Quarterbacks (Football)—United States—Biography—Juvenile literature.
4. Philanthropists—United States—Biography—Juvenile literature. I. Title.
  GV939.B685W55 2011
  796.332092—dc22
  [B]
                                 2010041784

122010 Lake Book Manufacturing, Inc., Melrose Park, IL

Printed in the United States of America

10 9 8 7 6 5 4 3 2 1

To Our Readers:
We have done our best to make sure all Internet addresses in this book were active and appropriate
when we went to press. However, the author and the publisher have no control over and assume
no liability for the material available on those Internet sites or on other Web sites they may link to.
Any comments or suggestions can be sent by e-mail to comments@enslow.com or to the address
on the back cover.

♻ Enslow Publishers, Inc., is committed to printing our books on recycled paper. The paper in
every book contains 10% to 30% post-consumer waste (PCW). The cover board on the outside
of each book contains 100% PCW. Our goal is to do our part to help young people and the
environment too!

Illustration Credits: Associated Press

Cover Illustration: Associated Press

Contents

Introduction

When the Associated Press was honoring the best pro football player for the decade of 2000–09, it was an easy choice: Tom Brady.

Why Brady? How about three Super Bowl championships in his first four seasons as a starter and two Super Bowl MVP awards? How about the 2007 season in which the New England Patriots won every game, the first team to go 16–0 in the regular season? How about Brady's record 50 touchdown passes that year, when New England scored 589 points, more than any team in history? He was the league's Most Valuable Player, too.

Not only was Brady the most successful quarterback in the NFL, but his team was at the top more than any other, winning the league title for the 2001, 2003, and 2004 seasons and playing for the 2007 championship, which the Patriots lost to the New York Giants.

Brady seemed to do it all with ease.

"He makes it look easy, but nobody works harder or gets everyone else to work harder the way Tom does," says Wes Welker, a record-setting receiver for the Patriots. "Tom's a great player and a great leader for all of us."

Brady injured his knee in the 2008 season opener against Kansas City. He missed the rest of the year. Before this injury, he had started 111 of the 113 games he played, winning 87 of them. He also won his first 10 playoff starts.

When he came back in 2009, he led the Patriots back into the playoffs.

Imagine all of that from someone who barely got drafted in 2000 and was not even a regular for part of his college career. And now, he is known as "Tom Terrific."

Only the 1972 Miami Dolphins had won every game in an NFL regular season, going 14–0. Tom Brady and the New England Patriots were not even thinking about perfection when the 2007 schedule began.

By midseason, though, everyone was asking if

chapter 1

16–0 Season

Tom Brady throws a pass against the Cleveland Browns on October 7, 2007.

the Patriots could go 16–0; the schedule had been lengthened in 1978. And everyone was wondering if Brady and his team would ever stop scoring.

New England won its first eight games by a combined 331 points to 127. The closest score was 34–17 over Cleveland.

Brady already had 30 touchdown passes. The record for a whole season was Peyton Manning's 49. That mark was set in 2004.

Always the team man, Brady was not thinking about himself.

"They are always meaningful games when you play them, and 8–0 is great," he said. "But it really doesn't mean anything, doesn't guarantee us anything."

Especially with the next game against Manning and the defending champion Colts. Indianapolis had won 12 in a row, including beating the Patriots for the AFC title 9½ months earlier.

This game was close, and Brady even was intercepted twice. But he threw for three TDs,

Randy Moss catches a 65-yard pass from Tom Brady in the fourth quarter of the Patriot's game against the New York Giants on December 29, 2007. Both Moss and Brady broke records on the play.

two in the fourth quarter, in a 24–20 comeback win.

"We knew there would be close games, and it means a lot to win one like that," Brady said.

They would need to win a few more that way, with back-to-back three-point victories over Philadelphia and Baltimore. Still, New England kept winning. And Brady caught fire again. Soon, the Patriots were 15–0.

"It would be a great thing to do, but it's not our main goal," Brady said of going 16–0. "What we are after is the Super Bowl."

The final regular-season game was at the New York Giants, who already had made the playoffs. The Giants promised they would use their starters and push the Patriots to the limit.

Did they ever!

New York led by 12 points in the second half. But Brady hooked up with top target Randy Moss for a 65-yard score that set two records: Brady beat Manning's mark with his 50th touchdown

Tom Brady is lifted in the air by his teammates after his huge, 65-yard pass play against the Giants. Brady and Moss broke the records for touchdown passes and receptions, respectively, on the play. The Patriots also finished 16–0 with the victory.

pass, and Moss broke Jerry Rice's single-season record of 22 TD receptions.

The Patriots rallied for a 38–35 win and finished the season with an incredible 589 points.

"In this game of football, it's hard to go 16-and-0," Moss said. "As a football player and a fan of the game, my hat's off to this organization."

And hats off to Tom Terrific, who added NFL Most Valuable Player honors to the greatest season any quarterback ever had.

When Tom Brady was born on August 3, 1977, his parents already had three daughters. While his sisters always looked out for him, they also were normal siblings and Tom got his share of teasing from the girls.

He also tagged along to all of their games—

Chapter 2

Young Tom

Tom Brady and his father, Tom Sr., at a charity golf event in 2006.

sisters Maureen, Nancy, and Julie played on lots of teams—and Tom learned to love sports, too.

While at St. Gregory School in San Mateo, California, Tom began playing flag football, then youth football. His usual position: quarterback.

Lorraine Paul, the principal at St. Gregory, said Tom was smart and popular, which did not surprise her because "his older sisters were the same way."

He also liked to compete. His favorite sport was football because he often went to see 49ers games when San Francisco was winning Super Bowls.

"Joe Montana, Steve Young, Jerry Rice, those were my heroes," Brady said.

Before he would become a sports hero himself, Brady first had to become a starter at Junipero Serra High School. It did not take all that long. By the eleventh grade, Brady was one of California's best quarterbacks.

But Tom was also a very good baseball player (a catcher), and had a chance to try for the major

Tom Brady and teammate Otis Smith toss out ceremonial first pitches before a Boston Red Sox game in 2002. Brady nearly became a pro baseball player before deciding to stick with football.

leagues with the Montreal Expos. He thought about it, too, then stuck with his favorite sport and had a great senior football season for Serra High.

In all, Brady threw for 3,702 yards and 31 touchdowns in high school. That his record was just 11–9 as a starter did not stop dozens of colleges from trying to sign him, and he chose the University of Michigan, which has a history of strong quarterbacks.

Not that the folks in San Mateo expected Tom Brady to become, well, Tom Terrific. John Kirby, a receiver for Brady in high school, reflected, "You never think your high school quarterback, the guy who was throwing you passes, would become such a star."

om Brady joined the Michigan Wolverines at the right time. The university won the national championship in 1997, when Brady backed up Brian Griese. Then Griese went to the NFL and the quarterback's job was Brady's.

Soon after, Michigan's fans became unhappy.

Chapter 3

A Wolverine

The Wolverines lost to Notre Dame and then to Syracuse to open the 1998 season. When they fell behind, 38–7, to the Orange, Brady was replaced by freshman Drew Henson, who threw for three touchdowns.

As a young quarterback for the University of Michigan, Tom Brady is about to hand off the ball in a game against Michigan State in 1998.

Brady throws a pass against Penn State on November 7, 1998.

The fans wanted Henson to become the starter. Coach Lloyd Carr kept Brady in the lineup.

For the rest of that year and all of the next, Brady would hear boos when he played poorly, and people would call for him to be benched.

It did not happen.

The Wolverines quickly turned things around, winning ten of the next eleven games for a share of the Big 10 championship. They beat Arkansas in the Citrus Bowl as Brady took them on two late TD drives after his two interceptions put Michigan behind.

"The measure of a quarterback isn't statistics, but wins and getting your team in the end zone," Carr said. "This is what a quarterback lives for."

Still, Brady would have to live through many more calls for Henson to be the No. 1 quarterback. He even thought about going to another school. But Carr stuck with Brady, although both QBs played in 1999 as the Wolverines went 10–2.

Brady's final game for Michigan was his best. Twice, he brought his team back from fourteen-

Brady practices his throws as he prepares to face off against Arkansas in the Citrus Bowl on New Year's Day, 1999.

point holes in the Orange Bowl. In overtime, his TD pass to Shawn Thompson beat Alabama, 35–34.

"That's what Brady is all about and that's what Michigan is all about," Carr said. "He's a special guy."

Overall, Brady was 20–5 as a starter in college, yet he was not a top prospect for NFL teams. He was not drafted until the sixth round in April 2000, by New England at the 199th overall spot.

It would turn out to be one of the smartest picks in football history.

"GET BRADY OUT THERE!"

Not the words Tom Brady expected to hear in the second game of the 2001 season. Sure, he had gone from sixth-round draft pick and third-stringer to backup quarterback behind Drew Bledsoe.

Chapter 4

Suddenly a Star

Brady prepares to throw a deep pass against the New York Jets on December 2, 2001.

But Brady was unproven and Bledsoe was a veteran starter.

Then Bledsoe injured his chest against the New York Jets, and the coaches were yelling for Brady to get on the field.

New England lost that game, and as Brady grew into the job while Bledsoe was out, the Patriots were 5–5.

Brady played like a veteran and was not intercepted in his first 162 throws, an NFL record. He led the Patriots to six straight wins to close the 2001 season and win the AFC East.

"I sure hope there are bigger days ahead in bigger arenas," Brady said.

There would be. And Brady would be the headliner.

New England opened the playoffs against Oakland on a snowy Saturday night. The Raiders led, 13–10, with 1:43 left when Brady fumbled while being sacked. But the officials looked at video replay and changed it to an incompletion

Brady leads the Pats on a drive against the St. Louis Rams in Super Bowl XXXVI.

because Brady's arm was coming forward as he tried to tuck in the ball.

That play became famous as the tuck rule, and it helped New England tie the game, then win it in overtime.

Brady became well known for that play—at least until he did something far more special a few weeks later.

The Patriots needed Bledsoe in the next game when Brady sprained his ankle, and Bledsoe helped them beat Pittsburgh to reach the Super Bowl. Coach Bill Belichick said if Brady was healthy, he would start against the heavily favored St. Louis Rams.

Brady was healthy—and wide-eyed about his first Super Bowl week.

"You know the Super Bowl is a big deal, but when you get a chance to play in it and see everything going on, it's even bigger than you can imagine," Brady said.

Few people imagined the Patriots staying close to the Rams, but New England's defense

Brady rides in a parade at Disney World the day after winning his first Super Bowl with the New England Patriots.

confused quarterback Kurt Warner, the league's MVP. Brady took a nap on the locker-room floor before the game, then stayed cool and helped his team build a 17–3 lead.

Warner rallied St. Louis into a tie, setting up Brady's first of many star turns.

With no time-outs and 1:21 remaining, Brady hit on five passes as New England marched from its 17-yard line to Adam Vinatieri's 48-yard field goal on the final play. For leading the huge upset, Brady was chosen Super Bowl MVP.

He was the biggest star in America's biggest game.

Achampionship in his second pro season was just the start for Tom Brady. Two years later, he guided the Patriots to a 14–2 record, best in the league. Not yet a great passer, Brady remained an excellent leader.

"The mark of a great player is how well you

Chapter 5

Tom Terrific

play over time," Brady said. "That's the goal, to be dependable, to be consistent."

His teammates knew they could most depend on Brady in the playoffs. He helped them beat Tennessee in the bitter cold, then Indianapolis, to

Tom Brady tries to avoid the onrushing defense of the Carolina Panthers during Super Bowl XXXVIII.

reach the Super Bowl. Once there, it was time for Tom to be terrific.

He had the best playoff game of his early career against Carolina in a 32–29 victory. His 32 completions and 3 TD passes earned him Super Bowl MVP honors again. And like he did against the Rams two years before, Brady led New England on a drive to Adam Vinatieri's winning field goal as the game ended.

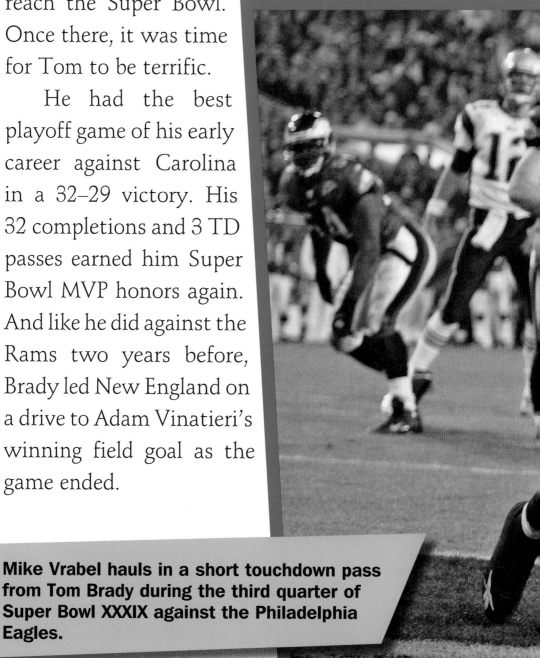

Mike Vrabel hauls in a short touchdown pass from Tom Brady during the third quarter of Super Bowl XXXIX against the Philadelphia Eagles.

Brady now was a celebrity, getting invited to the White House and to Disney World. He soon would be hosting TV shows and appearing in commercials.

"It's been a great couple of years," he said. "But when that success on the football field goes away, so do all the really neat things I get to do. That's why football is always going to be No. 1."

Could the Patriots stay No. 1 the next year? You bet.

After winning their final twelve games of 2003, they won six straight to start 2004. The 18-game winning string was a record (New England would break it a few years later, as would Indianapolis), and the Pats went 14–2 again.

Once again, they won a close Super Bowl as Brady lifted his postseason record to 9–0. Their 24–21 victory over Philadelphia gave Brady three titles in five NFL seasons, better than many Hall-of-Fame quarterbacks.

The Patriots also had changed from a running offense to more of a passing game. Thanks to

Brady holds up the Super Bowl trophy after the Pats beat the Eagles in Super Bowl XXXIX. This was the team's third championship in four seasons.

Brady, they now could outscore anybody through the air, and soon he would be setting records and leading his team to a 21-game winning streak.

"Tom Brady is the greatest winner in football right now. I don't care what anybody says," teammate Ty Law said. "Maybe his numbers are not eye-popping—all these yards, all these touchdowns—but he knows how to win ballgames."

When Tom Brady's sister Nancy went to Uganda to work with some of the world's poorest children, the quarterback decided to buy laptops as part of the "One Laptop Per Child" effort in the African country.

"After meeting with the group, I committed

Chapter 6

Making a Difference

Brady is introduced by Best Buddies participant Katie Meade during an event to benefit Best Buddies International.

to buying 1,500 laptops and sending them to my amazing sister . . . doing a mission in Uganda," Brady said. Nancy hand delivered them to the youngsters.

Tom wanted to help "carry out this wonderful charity's vision to give every child a chance to connect with the rest of the world no matter their personal circumstances."

Brady remains involved with Junípero Serra High School where he was a football star. After he was given a Cadillac convertible for being Super Bowl MVP in 2004, he donated the car as part of a school raffle—and the school raised $367,000 overall in the raffle. Brady also signed two hundred footballs for students who had sold raffle tickets.

One of Brady's favorite charities is Best Buddies. He has served as the honorary chairman for the annual Best Buddies Challenge, a cycling event that raises money for the group. Best Buddies gives mentally and physically challenged

Brady golfs with former presidents George H. W. Bush and Bill Clinton during a fund-raiser in 2006.

people a chance to make friends and find jobs. It was begun by the Kennedy and Shriver families.

Through Goodwill of Boston, Brady and Patriots teammates have served food to the homeless on Thanksgiving Day. Recently, Brady's wife, world-famous model Gisele Bundchen, has joined them to serve turkey and dessert.

Brady also enjoys spending time with his family. His first, son, John Edward Thomas Moynahan, was born in August 2007. Gisele and Brady were married in February 2009. In December, Brady and Gisele welcomed his second son, Benjamin Rein Brady.

On March 27, 2010, Brady helped the World Wildlife Fund (WWF) promote Earth Hour. He made a public service announcement asking people to turn off their lights for one hour. Bundchen also filmed an ad for Earth Hour.

Nearly one billion people took part in the event, the WWF said.

"Helping out is something I have always believed is important," Brady said. "I'm happy to do it and happy to have the opportunity to do it."

Career Statistics

Year	Team	Games	Att	Comp	Pct	Yds	Td	Int
2000	Patriots	1	3	1	33.3	6	0	0
2001	Patriots	15	413	264	63.9	2,843	18	12
2002	Patriots	16	601	373	62.1	3,764	28	14
2003	Patriots	16	527	317	60.2	3,620	23	12
2004	Patriots	16	474	288	60.8	3,692	28	14
2005	Patriots	16	530	334	63.0	4,110	26	14
2006	Patriots	16	516	319	61.8	3,529	24	12
2007	Patriots	16	578	398	68.9	4,806	50	8
2008	Patriots	1	11	7	63.6	76	0	0
2009	Patriots	16	565	371	65.7	4,398	28	13
	TOTALS	129	4,218	2,672	63.3	30,844	225	99

Att = Attempts   Pct = Completion Percentage   Td = Touchdowns
Comp = Completions   Yds = Yards   Int = Interceptions

Where to Write

TOM BRADY
C/O NEW ENGLAND PATRIOTS
One Patriot Place
Foxborough, MA 02035

All-Pro—One of the best players in the league as selected by member of the Associated Press.

block—How players get in the way of other players.

center—The player who hikes the ball to the quarterback and is also the leader of the offensive line.

defense—The act of stopping the other team from scoring.

end zone—Where teams try to advance the ball to score points.

field goal—A kick, worth three points, that goes through the goalposts.

freshman—Someone in his or her first year of high school or college.

goalposts—The posts at the back of the end zone. Kicks through them are worth either one point (after a touchdown and called an extra point) or three points (called a field goal).

home-field advantage—A team playing at its own stadium. Many teams play better at home than away.

linebacker—A position on defense from which players make tackles or cover receivers.

Most Valuable Player (MVP)—Award given to the best player in the league or game.

National Football League (NFL)—The thirty-two-team league for pro football.

playoffs—A series of games played after the regular season to determine a league champion.

quarterback—The player who takes the snap from the center and either hands off, runs himself, or throws the ball to other players. Sometimes he is referred to as the "field general" because he is in charge.

rookie—A first-year player.

running back—The player who takes handoffs from the quarterback and runs with the ball.

sack—When a quarterback is knocked to the ground before he can pass the ball.

Super Bowl—The championship game of pro football.

tackle—How players are knocked to the ground.

tight end—The player who stands at the end of the offensive line and either blocks or goes downfield to catch passes.

touchdown—When a player gets into the end zone with the ball, worth six points.

tuck rule—A special rule that helps determine whether a pass is either a fumble or simply incomplete.

veteran—A player with years of experience.

wide receiver—The player who stands to the outside when the ball is snapped and usually catches passes.

winning record—When a team has more wins than losses in a season.

Books

Ritchey, Kate. *Tom Brady: Champion Teammate*. New York: Grosset & Dunlap, 2008.

Savage, Jeff. *Tom Brady*. Minneapolis: First Avenue Editions, 2008.

Stewart, Mark. *Tom Brady: Heart of the Huddle*. Brookfield, Conn.: Millbrook Press, Inc., 2003.

Internet Addresses

Tom Brady's Official Web Site
http://www.tombrady.com

Official Web Site of the New England Patriots
http://www.patriots.com

NFL Official Site
http://www.nfl.com

Index